To _____

From _____

Great is the power of might and mind,
But only love can make us kind,
And only love can completely fill
The hearts of all with peace and goodwill.

The Helen Steiner Rice Foundation

When someone does a kindness
it always seems to me
That's the way God up in heaven
would like us all to be . . .

Whatever the celebration, whatever the day, whatever the event, whatever the occasion, Helen Steiner Rice possessed the ability to express the appropriate feeling for that particular moment. A happening became happier, a sentiment more sentimental, a memory more memorable because of her deep sensitivity and ability to put into understandable language the emotion being experienced. Her positive attitude, her concern for others, and her love of God are identifiable threads woven into her life, her work . . . and even her death.

Prior to Mrs. Rice's passing, she established the HELEN STEINER RICE FOUNDATION, a nonprofit corporation that awards grants to worthy charitable programs assisting the elderly and the needy.

Royalties from the sale of this book will add to the financial capabilities of the HELEN STEINER RICE FOUNDATION. Because of limited resources, the foundation presently limits grants to qualified charitable programs in Lorain, Ohio, where Helen Steiner Rice was born, and Greater Cincinnati, Ohio, where Mrs. Rice lived and worked most of her life. Hopefully in the future, resources will be of sufficient size that broader geographical areas may be considered in the awarding of grants.

Because of her foresight, caring, and deep conviction of sharing, Helen Steiner Rice continues to touch a countless number of lives through foundation grants and through her inspirational poetry.

Thank you for your assistance in helping to keep Helen's dream alive and growing.

Andrea E. Cornett, Administrator

Stan Myers is an award-winning artist and member of the prestigious National Watercolor Society. His work is included in both private and corporate collections and represented by several galleries in the Midwest.

Someone Cares

Helen Steiner Rice

Fleming H. Revell
A Division of Baker Book House
Grand Rapids, Michigan 49516

Published by Fleming H. Revell
a division of Baker Book House Company
P.O. Box 6287, Grand Rapids, MI 49516-6287

First edition published 1972

Printed in the United States of America

Library of Congress Cataloging-in-Publication Data

Rice, Helen Steiner.
   Someone cares / Helen Steiner Rice.
    p. cm.
   ISBN 0-8007-1748-1 (hardcover)
   1. Christian poetry, American. I. Title.
PS3568.I28S6 1998
811'.54—dc21   98-12885

For current information about all releases from Baker Book House, visit our web site:
                   http://www.bakerbooks.com

Contents

Someone Cares

Someone cares and always will,
The world forgets, but God loves you still.
You cannot go beyond His love
No matter what you're guilty of—
For God forgives until the end,
He is your faithful, loyal friend,
And though you try to hide your face
There is no shelter any place
That can escape His watchful eye,
For on the earth and in the sky
He's ever present and always there
To take you in His tender care
And bind the wounds and mend the breaks
When all the world around forsakes.
Someone cares and loves you still,
And God is the someone who always will.

He Loves You

I'm way down here!
  You're way up there!
Are You sure You can hear
  my faint, faltering prayer?
For I'm so unsure
  of just how to pray—
To tell You the truth, God,
  I don't know what to say.
I just know I am lonely
  and vaguely disturbed,
Bewildered and restless,
  confused and perturbed.
And they tell me that prayer
  helps to quiet the mind
And to unburden the heart
  for in stillness we find
A newborn assurance
  that someone does care
And someone does answer
  each small, sincere prayer.

Be of Good Cheer

Cheerful thoughts like sunbeams
  lighten up the darkest fears,
For when the heart is happy
  there's just no time for tears,
And when the face is smiling
  it's impossible to frown,
And when you are high-spirited
  you cannot feel low-down,
For the nature of our attitude
  toward circumstantial things
Determines our acceptance
  of the problems that life brings,
And since fear and dread and worry
  cannot help in any way,
It's much healthier and happier
  to be cheerful every day.
And if you'll only try it
  you will find, without a doubt,
A cheerful attitude's something
  no one should be without,
For when the heart is cheerful
  it cannot be filled with fear,
And without fear the way ahead
  seems more distinct and clear,
And we realize there's nothing
  we need ever face alone
For our heavenly Father loves us
  and our problems are His own.

The Spider
and the Silken Strand

There's an old Danish legend
  with a lesson for us all
Of an ambitious spider
  and his rise and his fall,
Who wove his sheer web
  with intricate care
As it hung suspended
  somewhere in midair.
Then in soft, idle luxury
  he feasted each day
On the small, foolish insects
  he enticed as his prey,
Growing ever more arrogant
  and smug all the while
He lived like a king
  in self-satisfied style.
And gazing one day
  at the sheer strand suspended,
He said, "I don't need this,"
  so he recklessly rended
The strand that had held
  his web in its place
And with sudden swiftness
  the web crumpled in space.
And that was the end
  of the spider who grew
So arrogantly proud
  that he no longer knew

That it was the strand
    that reached down from above
Like the chord of God's grace
    and His infinite love.
And this old legend
    with simplicity told
Is a moral as true
    as the legend is old—
Don't sever the lifeline
    that links you to
The Father in heaven
    who cares for you.

It's a Wonderful World

In spite of the fact
    we complain and lament
And view this old world
    with much discontent,
Deploring conditions
    and grumbling because
There's so much injustice
    and so many flaws,
It's a wonderful world
    and it's people like you
Who make it that way
    by the things that you do—
For a warm, ready smile
    or a kind, thoughtful deed,
Or a hand outstretched
    in an hour of need
Can change our whole outlook
    and make the world bright
Where a minute before
    just nothing seemed right.
It's a wonderful world
    and it always will be
If we keep our eyes open
    and focused to see
The wonderful things
    we are capable of
When we open our hearts
    to God and His love.

God Loves You

It's amazing and incredible,
    but it's as true as it can be,
God loves and understands us all
    and that means you and me—
His grace is all sufficient
    for both the young and old,
For the lonely and the timid,
    for the brash and for the bold—
His love knows no exceptions,
    so never feel excluded,
No matter who or what you are,
    your name has been included.
And no matter what your past has been,
    trust God to understand,
And no matter what your problem is,
    just place it in His hand,
For in all of our unloveliness
    this great God loves us still,
He loved us since the world began
    and what's more, He always will.

Good Morning, God!

You are ushering in another day
   untouched and freshly new,
So here I come to ask You, God,
   if You'll renew me too.
Forgive the many errors
   that I made yesterday
And let me try again, dear God,
   to walk closer in Your way.
But, Father, I am well aware
   I can't make it on my own,
So take my hand and hold it tight
   for I can't walk alone.

The Peace of Meditation

So we may know God better
  and feel His quiet power,
Let us daily keep in silence
  a meditation hour—
For to understand God's greatness
  and to use His gifts each day
The soul must learn to meet Him
  in a meditative way,
For our Father tells His children
  that if they would know His will
They must seek Him in the silence
  when all is calm and still,
For nature's greatest forces
  are found in quiet things
Like softly falling snowflakes
  drifting down on angels' wings.
So let us plan with prayerful care
  to always allocate
A certain portion of each day
  to be still and meditate,
For when everything is quiet
  and we're lost in meditation,
Our soul is then preparing
  for a deeper dedication
That will make it wholly possible
  to quietly endure
The violent world around us—
  for in God we are secure.

No Favor Do I Seek Today

I come not to ask, to plead, or implore You,
I just come to tell You how much I adore You,
For to kneel in Your presence makes me feel blest
For I know that You know all my needs best.
And it fills me with joy just to linger with You
As my soul You replenish and my heart You renew,
For prayer is much more than just asking for things—
It's the peace and contentment that quietness brings.
So thank You again for Your mercy and love
And for making me heir to Your Kingdom above.

The Mystery of Prayer

Beyond that which words can interpret
    or theology can explain,
The soul feels a shower of refreshment
    that falls like the gentle rain
On hearts that are parched with problems
    and are searching to find the way
To somehow attract God's attention
    through well-chosen words as they pray,
Not knowing that God in His wisdom
    can sense all their worry and woe
For there is nothing they can conceal
    that God does not already know.
So kneel in prayer in His presence
    and you'll find no need to speak,
For softly in silent communion
    God grants you the peace that you seek.

It's Me Again, God

Remember me, God?
  I come every day
Just to talk with You, Lord,
  and to learn how to pray.
You make me feel welcome,
  You reach out Your hand,
I need never explain
  for You understand.
I come to You frightened
  and burdened with care,
So lonely and lost
  and so filled with despair,
And suddenly, Lord,
  I'm no longer afraid,
My burden is lighter
  and the dark shadows fade.
Oh, God, what a comfort
  to know that You care
And to know when I seek You,
  You will always be there.

What Is Prayer?

Is it measured words that are memorized,
Forcefully said and dramatized,
Offered with pomp and with arrogant pride
In words unmatched to the feeling inside?
No . . . prayer is so often just words unspoken,
Whispered in tears by a heart that is broken,
For God is already deeply aware
Of the burdens we find too heavy to bear,
And all we need do is to seek Him in prayer
And without a word He will help us to bear
Our trials and troubles, our sickness and sorrow,
And show us the way to a brighter tomorrow.
There's no need at all for impressive prayer,
For the minute we seek God He is already there.

Meet God in the Morning

"The earth is the Lord's
    and the fullness thereof"—
It speaks of His greatness,
    it sings of His love,
And each day at dawning
    I lift my heart high
And raise up my eyes
    to the infinite sky.
I watch the night vanish
    as a new day is born,
And I hear the birds sing
    on the wings of the morn.
I see the dew glisten
    in crystal-like splendor
While God, with a touch
    that is gentle and tender,
Wraps up the night
    and softly tucks it away
And hangs out the sun
    to herald a new day.
And so I give thanks
    and my heart kneels to pray—
"God, keep me and guide me
    and go with me today."

Help Yourself to Happiness

Everybody, everywhere
   seeks happiness, it's true,
But finding it and keeping it
   seems difficult to do,
Difficult because we think
   that happiness is found
Only in the places where
   wealth and fame abound.
And so we go on searching
   in palaces of pleasure,
Seeking recognition
   and monetary treasure,
Unaware that happiness
   is just a state of mind
Within the reach of everyone
   who takes time to be kind,
For in making others happy
   we will be happy too,
For the happiness you give away
   returns to shine on you.

The World
Would Be a Nicer Place

Amid stresses and strains
   much too many to mention,
And pressure-packed days
   filled with turmoil and tension,
We seldom have time
   to be friendly or kind
For we're harassed and hurried
   and always behind.
And while we've more gadgets
   and buttons to press,
Making leisure hours greater
   and laboring hours less,
And our standards of living
   they claim have improved,
And repressed inhibitions
   have been freed and removed,
It seems all this progress
   and growth are for naught,
For daily we see
   a world more distraught.
So what does it matter
   if we reach our goals
And gain the whole world
   but lose our souls,
For what have we won
   if in gaining this end
We've been much too busy
   to be kind to a friend?

And what is there left
    to make the heart sing
When life is a cold
    and mechanical thing
And we are but puppets
    of controlled automation
Instead of joint heirs
    to God's gift of creation?

He Asks So Little
and Gives So Much

What must I do
   to insure peace of mind?
Is the answer I'm seeking
   too hard to find?
How can I know
   what God wants me to be?
How can I tell
   what's expected of me?
Where can I go
   for guidance and aid
To help me correct
   the errors I've made?
The answer is found
   in doing three things
And great is the gladness
   that doing them brings—
"Do justice, love kindness,
   walk humbly with God,"
For with these three things
   as your rule and your rod,
All things worth having
   are yours to achieve
If you follow God's words
   and have faith to believe.

Things to Be Thankful For

The good, green earth beneath our feet,
The air we breathe, the food we eat,
Some work to do, a goal to win,
A hidden longing deep within
That spurs us on to bigger things
And helps us meet what each day brings—
All these things and many more
Are things we should be thankful for . . .
And most of all our thankful prayers
Should rise to God because He cares.

Look on the Sunny Side

There are always two sides,
  the good and the bad,
The dark and the light,
  the sad and the glad.
And in counting our blessings
  we find when we're through
We've no reason at all
  to complain or be blue.
So thank God for good things
  He has already done,
And be grateful to Him
  for the battles you've won,
And know that the same God
  who helped you before
Is ready and willing
  to help you once more.
Then with faith in your heart
  reach out for God's hand
And accept what He sends,
  though you can't understand,
For our Father in heaven
  always knows what is best,
And if you trust in His wisdom
  your life will be blest,
For always remember
  that whatever betide you,
You are never alone
  for God is beside you.

A Sure Way to a Happy Day

Happiness is something
   we create in our mind,
It's not something we search for
   and so seldom find.
It's just waking up
   and beginning the day
By counting our blessings
   and kneeling to pray—
It's giving up thoughts
   that breed discontent
And accepting what comes
   as a gift heaven sent—
It's giving up wishing
   for things we have not
And making the best of
   whatever we've got—
It's knowing that life
   is determined for us,
And pursuing our tasks
   without fret, fume, or fuss—
For it's by completing
   what God gives us to do
That we find real contentment
   and happiness too.

The Golden Chain

Friendship is a golden chain,
  the links are friends so dear,
And like a rare and precious jewel
  it's treasured more each year.
It's clasped together firmly
  with a love that's deep and true,
And it's rich with happy memories
  and fond recollections too.
Time can't destroy its beauty
  for as long as memory lives,
Years can't erase the pleasure
  that the joy of friendship gives,
For friendship is a priceless gift
  that can't be bought or sold,
But to have an understanding friend
  is worth far more than gold.
And the golden chain of friendship
  is a strong and blessed tie
Binding kindred hearts together
  as the years go passing by.

The Gift of Friendship

Friendship is a priceless gift
    that can't be bought or sold,
But its value is far greater
    than a mountain made of gold—
For gold is cold and lifeless,
    it can neither see nor hear,
And in the time of trouble
    it is powerless to cheer.
It has no ears to listen,
    no heart to understand,
It cannot bring you comfort
    or reach out a helping hand.
So when you ask God for a gift,
    be thankful if He sends
Not diamonds, pearls, or riches,
    but the love of real true friends.

Give Us Daily Awareness

On life's busy thoroughfares
We meet with angels unawares—
So, Father, make us kind and wise
So we may always recognize
The blessings that are ours to take,
The friendships that are ours to make
If we but open our heart's door wide
To let the sunshine of love inside.

A Friend Is a Gift of God

Among the great and glorious gifts
  our heavenly Father sends
Is the gift of understanding
  that we find in loving friends,
For in this world of trouble
  that is filled with anxious care,
Everybody needs a friend
  in whom they're free to share
The little secret heartaches
  that lay heavy on their mind,
Not just a mere acquaintance
  but someone who's just our kind.
For somehow in the generous heart
  of loving, faithful friends,
The good God in His charity
  and wisdom always sends
A sense of understanding
  and the power of perception
And mixes these fine qualities
  with kindness and affection.
So when we need some sympathy
  or a friendly hand to touch,
Or an ear that listens tenderly
  and speaks words that mean so much,
We seek our true and trusted friend
  in the knowledge that we'll find
A heart that's sympathetic
  and an understanding mind.

Strangers Are Friends
We Haven't Met

God knows no strangers, He loves us all—
    the poor, the rich, the great, the small.
He is a friend who is always there
    to share our troubles and lessen our care.
No one is a stranger in God's sight,
    for God is love and in His light
May we too try in our small way
    to make new friends from day to day.
So pass no stranger with an unseeing eye,
    for God may be sending a new friend by.

The Key to Living Is Giving

A very favorite story of mine
   is about two seas in Palestine—

One is a sparkling sapphire jewel,
   its waters are clean and clear and cool,
Along its shores the children play
   and travelers seek it on their way,
And nature gives so lavishly
   her choicest gems to the Galilee.
But on to the south the Jordan flows
   into a sea where nothing grows,
No splash of fish, no singing bird,
   no children's laughter is ever heard.
The air hangs heavy all around
   and nature shuns this barren ground.
Both seas receive the Jordan's flow,
   the water is just the same, we know,
But one of the seas, like liquid sun,
   can warm the hearts of everyone,
While farther south another sea
   is dead and dark and miserly—
It takes each drop the Jordan brings
   and to each drop it fiercely clings,
It hoards and holds the Jordan's waves
   until like shackled, captured slaves,
The fresh, clear Jordan turns to salt
   and dies within the Dead Sea's vault.
But the Jordan flows on rapturously
   as it enters and leaves the Galilee,

For every drop that the Jordan gives
    becomes a laughing wave that lives—
For the Galilee gives back each drop,
    its waters flow and never stop,
And in this laughing, living sea
    that takes and gives so generously
We find the key to life and living
    is not in keeping but in giving.

Yes, there are two Palestinian seas
    and mankind is fashioned after these.

Everyone Needs Someone

People need people and friends need friends,
And we all need love for a full life depends
Not on vast riches or great acclaim,
Not on success or on worldly fame,
But just in knowing that someone cares
And holds us close in their thoughts and prayers—
For only the knowledge that we're understood
Makes everyday living feel wonderfully good.
And we rob ourselves of life's greatest need
When we lock up our hearts and fail to heed
The outstretched hand reaching to find
A kindred spirit whose heart and mind
Are lonely and longing to somehow share
Our joys and sorrows and to make us aware
That life's completeness and richness depends
On the things we share with our loved ones and friends.

Thank You, God, for Everything

Thank You, God, for everything—
    the big things and the small,
For every good gift comes from God,
    the giver of them all.
And all too often we accept
    without any thanks or praise
The gifts God sends as blessings
    each day in many ways.
So thank You for the little things
    that often come our way,
The things we take for granted
    but don't mention when we pray,
The unexpected courtesy,
    the thoughtful, kindly deed,
A hand reached out to help us
    in the time of sudden need.
Oh, make us more aware, dear God,
    of little daily graces
That come to us with sweet surprise
    from never-dreamed-of places.

When Things
Go Wrong

When you're troubled and worried and sick at heart
And your plans are upset and your world falls apart,
Remember God's ready and waiting to share
The burden you find much too heavy to bear—
So with faith, let go and let God lead the way
Into a brighter and less troubled day.

After the Winter,
God Sends the Spring

Springtime is a season
   of hope and joy and cheer,
There's beauty all around us
   to see and touch and hear.
So no matter how downhearted
   and discouraged we may be,
New hope is born when we behold
   leaves budding on a tree,
Or when we see a timid flower
   push through the frozen sod
And open wide in glad surprise
   its petaled eyes to God,
For this is just God saying,
   "Lift up your eyes to Me,
And the bleakness of your spirit,
   like the budding springtime tree,
Will lose its wintry darkness
   and your heavy heart will sing,"
For God never sends the winter
   without the joy of spring.

How Great the Yield
from a Fertile Field

The farmer ploughs through the fields of green
And the blade of the plough is sharp and keen,
But the seed must be sown to bring forth grain,
For nothing is born without suffering and pain,
And God never ploughs in the soul of man
Without intention and purpose and plan.
So whenever you feel the plough's sharp blade
Let not your heart be sorely afraid
For like the farmer God chooses a field
From which He expects an excellent yield—
So rejoice though your heart is broken in two,
God seeks to bring forth a rich harvest in you.

Great Faith Is Born
of Great Trials

It's easy to say "In God we trust"
    when life is radiant and fair,
But the test of faith is only found
    when there are burdens to bear.
For our claim to faith in the sunshine
    is really no faith at all,
For when roads are smooth and days are bright
    our need for God is so small.
And no one discovers the fullness
    or the greatness of God's love
Unless they have walked in the darkness
    with only a light from above.
For the faith to endure whatever comes
    is born of sorrow and trials
And strengthened only by discipline
    and nurtured by self-denials.
So be not disheartened by troubles,
    for trials are the building blocks
On which to erect a fortress of faith,
    secure on God's ageless rocks.

There Are Blessings
in Everything

Blessings come in many guises
That God alone in love devises.
And sickness which we dread so much
Can bring a very healing touch,
For often on the wings of pain
The peace we sought before in vain
Will come to us with sweet surprise
For God is merciful and wise—
And through long hours of tribulation
God gives us time for meditation,
And no sickness can be counted loss
That teaches us to bear our cross.

Trouble Is a Stepping-Stone to Growth

Trouble is something no one can escape—
Everyone has it in some form or shape.
Some people hide it way down deep inside,
Some people bear it with gallant-like pride.
Some people worry and complain of their lot,
Some people covet what they haven't got
While others rebel and become bitter and old
With hopes that are dead and hearts that are cold.
But the wise man accepts whatever God sends,
Willing to yield like a storm-tossed tree bends,
For trouble is part and parcel of life,
And no one can grow without struggle and strife.
So blest are the people who learn to accept
The trouble we try to escape and reject,
For in our acceptance we're given great grace
And courage and faith and the strength to face
The daily troubles that come to us all,
So we may learn to stand straight and tall—
For the grandeur of life is born of defeat,
For in overcoming we make life complete.

Before You Can Dry
Another's Tears

If my eyes are dry and I never weep,
How do I know when the hurt is deep?
If my heart is cold and it never bleeds,
How can I tell what my brother needs?
For when ears are deaf to the beggar's plea
And we close our eyes and refuse to see,
And we steel our hearts and harden our minds,
And we count it a weakness whenever we're kind,
We are no longer following the Father's way
Or seeking His guidance from day to day.
For without crosses to carry and burdens to bear,
We dance through a life that is frothy and fair,
And chasing the rainbow we have no desire
For roads that are rough and realms that are higher.
So spare me no heartache or sorrow, dear Lord,
For the heart that is hurt reaps the richest reward,
And God enters the heart that is broken with sorrow
As He opens the door to a brighter tomorrow,
For only through tears can we recognize
The suffering that lies in another's eyes.

The Windows
of Gold

There is a legend that has often been told
Of the boy who searched for the windows of gold,
The beautiful windows he saw far away
When he looked in the valley at sunrise each day.
So he planned by day and he dreamed by night
Of how he could reach the great shining light,
And one golden morning when dawn broke through
And the valley sparkled with diamonds of dew,
He started to climb down the mountainside
With the windows of gold as his goal and his guide.
He entered the peaceful valley town
Just as the golden sun went down,
But he seemed to have lost his guiding light,
The windows were dark that had once been bright,
And hungry and tired and lonely and cold,
He cried, "Won't you show me the windows of gold?"
Then he saw the sun going down in a great golden ball
That burnished the windows of his cabin so small.
The Kingdom of God with its great shining light,
Like the golden windows that shone so bright,
Is not a far distant place somewhere,
It's as close to you as a silent prayer—
And your search for God will end and begin
When you look for Him and find Him within.

Fulfillment

Apple blossoms bursting wide
  now beautify the tree
And make a springtime picture
  that is beautiful to see.
Oh, fragrant lovely blossoms,
  you'll make a bright bouquet
If I but break your branches
  from the apple tree today.
But if I break your branches
  and make your beauty mine,
You'll bear no fruit in season
  when severed from the vine.
And when we cut ourselves away
  from guidance that's divine,
Our lives will be as fruitless
  as the branch without the vine,
For as the flowering branches
  depend upon the tree
To nourish and fulfill them
  till they reach maturity,
We too must be dependent
  on our Father up above,
For we are but the branches
  and He's the tree of love.

The Heavens Declare
the Glory of God

You ask me how I know it's true
   that there is a living God—
A God who rules the universe,
   the sky, the sea, the sod;
A God who holds all creatures
   in the hollow of His hand;
A God who put infinity
   in one tiny grain of sand;
A God who made the seasons—
   winter, summer, fall, and spring—
And put His flawless rhythm
   into each created thing;
A God who hangs the sun out
   slowly with the break of day,
And gently takes the stars in
   and puts the night away;
A God whose mighty handiwork
   defies the skill of man,
For no architect can alter
   God's perfect master plan—
What better answers are there
   to prove His holy being
Than the wonders all around us
   that are ours just for the seeing.

Ideals Are like Stars

In this world of casual carelessness,
    it's discouraging to try
To keep our morals and standards
    and our ideals high.
But no life is worth the living
    unless it's built on truth,
And we lay our life's foundation
    in the golden years of youth.
So allow no one to stop you
    or hinder you from laying
A firm and strong foundation
    made of faith and love and praying.
And remember that ideals are like
    stars up in the sky—
You can never really reach them,
    hanging in the heavens high,
But like the mighty mariner
    who sailed the storm-tossed sea
And used the stars to chart his course
    with skill and certainty,
You too can chart your course in life
    with high ideals and love,
For high ideals are like the stars
    that light the sky above.

God Is Never
beyond Our Reach

No one ever sought the Father
   and found He was not there,
And no burden is too heavy
   to be lightened by a prayer.
No problem is too intricate
   and no sorrow that we face
Is too deep and devastating
   to be softened by His grace.
No trials and tribulations
   are beyond what we can bear
If we share them with our Father
   as we talk to Him in prayer.
And those of every color,
   every race, and every creed
Have but to seek the Father
   in their deepest hour of need.
God asks for no credentials,
   He accepts us with our flaws,
He is kind and understanding
   and He welcomes us because
We are His erring children
   and He loves us every one,
And He freely and completely
   forgives all that we've done,
Asking only if we're ready
   to follow where He leads,
Content that in His wisdom
   He will answer all our needs.

We Can't, but God Can

Why things happen as they do
   we do not always know,
And we cannot always fathom
   why our spirits sink so low.
We flounder in our dark distress,
   we are wavering and unstable,
But when we're most inadequate
   the Lord God's always able,
For though we are incapable,
   God's powerful and great,
And there's no darkness of the mind
   that God can't penetrate.
And all that is required of us
   whenever things go wrong
Is to trust in God implicitly
   with a faith that's deep and strong,
And while He may not instantly
   unravel all the strands
Of the tangled thoughts that trouble us,
   He completely understands,
And in His time, if we have faith,
   He will gradually restore
The brightness to our spirit
   that we've been longing for.
So remember there's no cloud too dark
   for God's light to penetrate
If we keep on believing
   and have faith enough to wait.

The Light
of the World

Oh, Father, up in heaven,
   we have wandered far away
From Jesus Christ, our Savior,
   who arose on Easter Day.
And the promise of salvation
   that You gave us when Christ died,
We have often vaguely questioned,
   even doubted and denied.
We've forgotten why You sent us
   Jesus Christ, Your only Son,
And in arrogance and ignorance,
   it's our will, not Thine, be done.
And, God, in Thy great wisdom,
   lead us in the way that's right,
And may the darkness of this world
   be conquered by Thy light.

Where Can We Find Him?

Where can we find the holy One?
Where can we see His only Son?
The wise men asked, and we're asking still,
Where can we find this man of goodwill?
Is He far away in some distant place,
Ruling unseen from His throne of grace?
Is there nothing on earth that we can see
To give us proof of eternity?

It's true we have never looked on His face,
But His likeness shines forth from every place,
For the hand of God is everywhere
Along life's busy thoroughfare,
And His presence can be felt and seen
Right in the midst of our daily routine—
The things we touch and see and feel
Are what make God so very real . . .
The silent stars in timeless skies,
The wonderment in children's eyes,
The gossamer wings of a hummingbird,
The joy that comes from a kindly word,
The autumn haze, the breath of spring,
The chirping song the crickets sing,
A rosebud in a slender vase,
A smile upon a friendly face.

In everything both great and small
We see the hand of God in all,
And every day, somewhere, someplace,
We see the likeness of His face,
For who can watch a new day's birth,
Or touch the warm, life-giving earth,
Or feel the softness of the breeze,
Or look at skies through lacy trees
And say they've never seen His face
Or looked upon His throne of grace?

He Was One of Us

He was born as little children are
   and lived as children do,
So remember that the Savior
   was once a child like you.
And remember that He lived on earth
   in the midst of sinful men,
And the problems of the present
   existed even then:
He was tempted, He was hungry,
   He was lonely, He was sad—
There's no sorrowful experience
   that the Savior has not had;
And in the end he was betrayed
   and even crucified,
For He was truly one of us—
   He lived on earth and died.
So do not heed the skeptics
   who are often heard to say,
"What does God up in heaven
   know of things we face today?"
For our Father up in heaven
   is very much aware
Of our failures and shortcomings
   and the burdens that we bear.
So whenever you are troubled
   put your problems in God's hand,
For He has faced all problems
   And He will understand.

In the Garden of Gethsemane

Before the dawn of Easter
   there came Gethsemane,
Before the resurrection
   there were hours of agony,
For there can be no crown of stars
   without a cross to bear,
And there is no salvation
   without faith and love and prayer,
And when we take our needs to God
   let us pray as did His Son
That dark night in Gethsemane—
   "Thy will, not mine, be done."

Why Should He Die for Such as I?

In everything both great and small
We see the hand of God in all,
And in the miracles of spring
When everywhere in everything
His handiwork is all around
And every lovely sight and sound
Proclaims the God of earth and sky,
I ask myself, "Just who am I
That God should send His only Son
That my salvation would be won
Upon a cross by a sinless man
To bring fulfillment to God's plan?"
For Jesus suffered, bled, and died
That sinners might be sanctified,
And to grant God's children such as I
Eternal life in that home on high.

The Way of the Cross

He carried the cross to Calvary,
Carried its burden for you and me.
There on the cross He was crucified
And, because He suffered and bled and died,
We know that whatever our cross may be,
It leads to God and eternity.
For who can hope for a crown of stars
Unless it is earned with suffering and scars,
For how could we face the living Lord
And rightfully claim His promised reward
If we have not carried our cross of care
And tasted the cup of bitter despair.
Let those who yearn for the pleasures of life,
And long to escape all suffering and strife,
Rush recklessly on to an empty goal
With never a thought of the spirit and soul,
But if you are searching to find the way
To life everlasting and eternal day,
With faith in your heart take the path He trod,
For the way of the cross is the way to God.

In God Is Our Strength

It's a troubled world we live in
    and we wish that we might find
Not only happiness of heart
    but longed-for peace of mind.
But where can we begin our search
    in the age of automation,
With neighbor against neighbor
    and nation against nation,
Where values have no permanence
    and change is all around
And everything is sinking sand
    and nothing solid ground?
Have we placed our faith in leaders
    unworthy of our trust?
Have we lost our own identity
    and allowed our souls to rust?

Have we forgotten Babylon
    and Egypt, Rome, and Greece,
And all the mighty rulers
    who lived by war, not peace,
Who built their thrones and empires
    on power and manmade things
And never knew God's greatness
    or that He was King of kings?
But we've God's Easter promise,
    so let us seek new goals
That open up new vistas
    for our eternal souls,
For our strength and our security
    lie not in earthly things,
But in Christ the Lord who died
    and rose as King of kings.

Life Is Forever

If we did not go to sleep at night,
We'd never awaken to see the light,
And the joy of watching a new day break
Or meeting the dawn by some quiet lake
Would never be ours unless we slept
While God and all His angels kept
A vigil through this little death
That's over with the morning's breath.
And death too is a time of sleeping,
For those who die are in God's keeping,
And there's a sunrise for each soul,
For life, not death, is God's promised goal.
So trust God's promise and doubt Him never,
For only through death can we live forever.

The Legend of the Raindrop

The legend of the raindrop
   has a lesson for us all
As it trembled in the heavens
   questioning whether it should fall—
For the glistening raindrop argued
   to the genie of the sky,
"I am beautiful and lovely
   as I sparkle here on high,
And hanging here I will become
   part of the rainbow's hue
And I'll shimmer like a diamond
   for all the world to view."
But the genie told the raindrop,
   "Do not hesitate to go,
For you will be more beautiful
   if you fall to earth below,
For you will sink into the soil
   and be lost a while from sight,
But when you reappear on earth,
   you'll be looked on with delight.
For you will be the raindrop
   that quenched the thirsty ground
And helped the lovely flowers
   to blossom all around,
And in your resurrection
   you'll appear in queenly clothes
With the beauty of the lily
   and the fragrance of the rose.

Then when you wilt and wither
you'll become part of the earth
And make the soil more fertile
and give new flowers birth."
For there is nothing ever lost
or eternally neglected,
For everything God ever made
is always resurrected.
So trust God's all-wise wisdom
and doubt the Father never,
For in His heavenly Kingdom,
there is nothing lost forever.

I Do Not Go Alone

If death should beckon me with outstretched hand
And whisper softly of an unknown land,
I shall not be afraid to go,
For though the path I do not know,
I take death's hand without a fear,
For He who safely brought me here
Will also take me safely back,
And though in many things I lack,
He will not let me go alone
Into the valley that's unknown.
So I reach out and take death's hand
And journey to the promised land.

Spring Awakens
What Autumn Puts to Sleep

A garden of asters of varying hues,
Crimson pinks and violet blues,
Blossoming in the hazy fall,
Wrapped in autumn's lazy pall—
But early frost stole in one night
And like a chilling, killing blight
It touched each pretty aster's head
And now the garden's still and dead
And all the lovely flowers that bloomed
Will soon be buried and entombed
In winter's icy shroud of snow
But oh, how wonderful to know
That after winter comes the spring
To breathe new life in everything,
And all the flowers that fell in death
Will be awakened by spring's breath,
For in God's plan both men and flowers
Can only reach bright, shining hours
By dying first to rise in glory
And prove again the Easter story.

Death Is a Doorway

On the wings of death
   the soul takes flight
Into the land
   where there is no night,
For those who believe
   what the Savior said
Will rise in glory
   though they be dead.
So death comes to us
   just to open the door
To the Kingdom of God
   and life evermore.

There's Always a Springtime

After the winter comes the spring
To show us again that in everything
There's always renewal divinely planned,
Flawlessly perfect, the work of God's hand.
And just like the seasons that come and go
When the flowers of spring lay buried in snow,
God sends to the heart in its winter of sadness
A springtime awakening of new hope and gladness,
And loved ones who sleep in a season of death
Will, too, be awakened by God's life-giving breath.

A Bend in the Road

When we feel we have nothing left to give
    and we are sure that the song has ended,
When our day seems over and the shadows fall
    and the darkness of night has descended,
Where can we go to find the strength
    to valiantly keep on trying,
Where can we find the hand that will dry
    the tears that the heart is crying?
There's but one place to go and that is to God,
    and dropping all pretense and pride,
We can pour out our problems without restraint
    and gain strength with Him at our side.

And together we stand at life's crossroads
  and view what we think is the end,
But God has a much bigger vision
  and He tells us it's only a bend,
For the road goes on and is smoother,
  and the pause in the song is a rest,
And the part that's unsung and unfinished
  is the sweetest and richest and best.
So rest and relax and grow stronger,
  let go and let God share your load,
Your work is not finished or ended,
  you've just come to a bend in the road.

A Child's Faith

"Jesus loves me, this I know,
   for the Bible tells me so"—
Little children ask no more,
   for love is all they're looking for,
And in a small child's shining eyes
   the faith of all the ages lies,
And tiny hands and tousled heads
   that kneel in prayer by little beds
Are closer to the dear Lord's heart
   and of His Kingdom more a part
Than we who search, and never find,
   the answers to our questioning mind.
For faith in things we cannot see
   requires a child's simplicity,
For lost in life's complexities
   we drift upon uncharted seas
And slowly faith disintegrates
   while wealth and power accumulates.
And the more we learn, the less we know,
   and the more involved our thinking grows,
And in our arrogance and pride
   no longer are we satisfied
To place our confidence and love
   with childlike faith in God above.
Oh, Father, grant once more to us
   a simple childlike faith and trust,
And with a small child's trusting eyes
   may we all come to realize
That faith alone can save our souls
   and lead us on to higher goals.

This I Believe

Somehow the world seems to be most deeply concerned and curiously interested in who we are. But who we are is of such small importance to God, for His deep concern is with what we are. And complete and full knowledge of what we are is known to God alone, for man's small, shallow judgments are so empty of the goodness and greatness of God's merciful love. And while man's motives and missions, his programs and projects, and his accomplishments and acclaim can make him successful and secure for him a listing in *Who's Who*, he remains unlisted in God's *Who's Who*, for great is the power of might and mind, but only love can make us kind. And all we are or hope to be is empty pride and vanity if love is not a part of all, for the greatest man is very small.

When I attended Sunday school, which is now much more than half a century ago, I used to sing, with all the joy that a child's heart can hold, "Jesus loves me," for I knew He loved me then and that He would love me forever. This same knowledge still suffices to fill me with the same childlike faith I possessed then, for I believe only a child can really know the greatness of God's love. I think that in searching and studying and using our manmade theories, we tend to destroy the power, the glory, the greatness, and most of all, the incomprehensible miracle of God and His Son.

I ask for no sensational, spectacular evidence or proof that God is my Father and that His Son, Jesus, loves me. I only know that He who brought me into this world will also take me safely back, for though there are many things I lack, He will not let me go alone into a land that is unknown. And with that knowledge I can travel happily on the highway to heaven and always with hurrying feet, for I know God will open new fields of usefulness for me, where there are no limitations, no handicaps, and no restrictions.

I just know everything that has ever happened in my life, whether it was good or bad, glad or sad, God sent it for a reason, and I truly believe with all my heart that God never makes mistakes. I never question what God sends, for I realize, when you question God, you lose the unquestionable power of faith and you no longer can enjoy its endless benefits.

I pray constantly, not always on my knees or at special places or at special times, nor do I use impressive words. I just keep up a running conversation with God, hour by hour and day by day. I talk to Him about everything, and I ask Him for nothing, except the joy of knowing Him better and loving Him more.

I am well aware that I cannot make it on my own, and I ask God to take my hand and hold it tight, for I cannot walk alone. Each day God only asks us to do our best, and then He will take over and do all the rest. And remember, God is always available and ready to help anyone who asks Him, for God is here . . . He's there . . . He's everywhere . . . He's as close to you as He is to me, and wherever you are, God is sure to be. And I want you to know that the poems I write are not mine alone. They belong to God and to the people I've known. And while I may never have met you face to face, in God's love and by His grace, our hearts and minds can meet and share my little poems of faith and prayer, and though we are oceans and miles apart, God unites us in spirit and heart.